Animals and
Their Senses/
Los sentidos
de los animales

ANIMAL SMELL/
EL OLFATO EN LOS ANIMALES

by/por Kirsten Hall

Reading consultant/Consultora de lectura: Susan Nations, M.Ed.,
author, literacy coach, consultant/autora, tutora de alfabetización, consultora

WEEKLY
READER
EARLY LEARNING LIBRARY

Please visit our web site at: www.earlyliteracy.cc
For a free color catalog describing Weekly Reader® Early Learning Library's list of high-quality books, call 1-877-445-5824 (USA) or 1-800-387-3178 (Canada). Weekly Reader® Early Learning Library's fax: (414) 336-0164.

Library of Congress Cataloging-in-Publication Data available upon request from the publisher. Fax (414) 336-0157 for the attention of the Publishing Records Department.

ISBN 0-8368-4816-0 (lib. bdg.)
ISBN 0-8368-4822-5 (softcover)

This North American edition first published in 2006 by
Weekly Reader® Early Learning Library
A Member of the WRC Media Family of Companies
330 West Olive Street, Suite 100
Milwaukee, WI 53212 USA

Weekly Reader® Early Learning Library Editor: Barbara Kiely Miller
Weekly Reader® Early Learning Library Art Direction: Tammy West
Weekly Reader® Early Learning Library Graphic Designer and Page Layout: Jenni Gaylord
Weekly Reader® Early Learning Library Translators: Tatiana Acosta and Guillermo Gutiérrez

Photo Credits
The publisher would like to thank the following for permission to reproduce their royalty-free photographs: AbleStock: Cover, 4, 5, 6, 8, 10, 12, 20; Corel: 11; Digital Vision: 14, 15, 16, 17, 18, 21; Fotosearch/ Brand X Pictures: Title page, 9, 13; Fotosearch/Digital Vision: 7; Fotosearch/image 100: 19

Printed in the United States of America

1 2 3 4 5 6 7 8 9 09 08 07 06 05

Note to Educators and Parents

Reading is such an exciting adventure for young children! They are beginning to integrate their oral language skills with written language. To encourage children along the path to early literacy, books must be colorful, engaging, and interesting; they should invite the young reader to explore both the print and the pictures.

Animals and Their Senses is a new series designed to help children read about the five senses in animals. In each book young readers will learn interesting facts about the bodies of some animals and how the featured sense works for them.

Each book is specially designed to support the young reader in the reading process. The familiar topics are appealing to young children and invite them to read — and reread — again and again. The full-color photographs and enhanced text further support the student during the reading process.

In addition to serving as wonderful picture books in schools, libraries, homes, and other places where children learn to love reading, these books are specifically intended to be read within an instructional guided reading group. This small group setting allows beginning readers to work with a fluent adult model as they make meaning from the text. After children develop fluency with the text and content, the book can be read independently. Children and adults alike will find these books supportive, engaging, and fun!

— Susan Nations, M.Ed., author/literacy coach/reading consultant

Nota para los educadores y los padres

¡Leer es una aventura tan emocionante para los niños pequeños! A esta edad están comenzando a integrar su manejo del lenguaje oral con el lenguaje escrito. Para animar a los niños en el camino de la lectura incipiente, los libros deben ser coloridos, estimulantes e interesantes; deben invitar a los jóvenes lectores a explorar la letra impresa y las ilustraciones.

Los sentidos de los animales es una nueva colección diseñada para que los niños lean textos sobre los cinco sentidos en los animales. En cada libro, los jóvenes lectores aprenderán datos interesantes del cuerpo de algunos animales y cómo éstos usan el sentido que se presenta.

Cada libro está especialmente diseñado para ayudar a los jóvenes lectores en el proceso de lectura. Los temas familiares llaman la atención de los niños y los invitan a leer — y releer — una y otra vez. Las fotografías a todo color y el tamaño de la letra ayudan aún más al estudiante en el proceso de lectura.

Además de servir como maravillosos libros ilustrados en escuelas, bibliotecas, hogares y otros lugares donde los niños aprenden a amar la lectura, estos libros han sido especialmente concebidos para ser leídos en un grupo de lectura guiada. Este contexto permite que los lectores incipientes trabajen con un adulto que domina la lectura mientras van determinando el significado del texto. Una vez que los niños dominan el texto y el contenido, el libro puede ser leído de manera independiente. ¡Estos libros les resultarán útiles, estimulantes y divertidos a niños y a adultos por igual!

— Susan Nations, M.Ed., autora/tutora de alfabetización/consultora de desarrollo de la lectura

People use their noses to smell. **Scents**, or smells, are carried through the air. They enter the holes in our noses, or **nostrils**, when we breathe.

- - - - - - - - -

Las personas usamos nuestra nariz para oler. Los olores viajan por el aire. Cuando respiramos, los olores entran por los agujeros de la nariz, o **fosas nasales**.

Flowers and warm cookies have good smells. Dirty sneakers and garbage have bad smells.

– – – – – – – – –

Las flores y las galletas recién horneadas huelen bien. Las zapatillas de deporte sucias y la basura huelen mal.

Most kinds of animals smell with their noses, too. A polar bear can smell **prey** even in the snow.

La mayoría de los animales también huelen con la nariz. El oso polar puede oler a su **presa** hasta en la nieve.

A squirrel buries nuts and seeds in the ground. It uses its sense of smell to find them again.

– – – – – – – –

La ardilla entierra nueces y semillas en el suelo. Usa su sentido del olfato para volverlas a encontrar.

trunk/trompa

An elephant's nostrils are at the end of its trunk. An elephant remembers other elephants by their scents.

- - - - - - - - -

El elefante tiene las fosas nasales en la punta de la trompa. Los elefantes se reconocen unos a otros por el olor.

A hippo can smell the air even when it swims. Its nose often stays above the water.

－－－－－－－－

El hipopótamo puede oler el aire mientras nada. Su nariz se queda a menudo fuera del agua.

A shark has small nostrils, but it has a strong sense of smell. It can smell other animals that are far away.

– – – – – – – –

El tiburón tiene las fosas nasales pequeñas, pero su sentido del olfato es muy sensible. Puede oler animales que están lejos.

A wolf can smell better than a shark can. A wolf can smell a deer across a huge forest.

- - - - - - - - -

El olfato del lobo es mejor que el del tiburón. Un lobo puede oler a un venado que esté al otro lado de un bosque enorme.

A cat has an excellent sense of smell. It can smell about fourteen times better than a human can.

- - - - - - - -

Los gatos tienen un sentido del olfato excelente. Su olfato es catorce veces más sensible que el de un humano.

A dog can smell many things that people cannot smell. Some dogs can follow scents that are days old.

- - - - - - - - -

Un perro puede oler muchos olores que las personas no pueden percibir. Algunos perros son capaces de seguir el olor que dejó algo hace días.

A lizard does not smell with its nostrils. It smells with the **roof**, or top, of its mouth.

— — — — — — — —

El lagarto no huele con las fosas nasales. Huele con el **cielo**, o parte superior, de la boca.

tongue/lengua

A snake also smells with the roof of its mouth. First, it grabs scents from the air with its tongue.

━ ━ ━ ━ ━ ━ ━ ━ ━

La serpiente también huele con el cielo de la boca. Primero, atrapa los olores del aire con la lengua.

Ants use smells to tell each other things. They find food by following scents left behind by other ants.

— — — — — — — — —

Las hormigas usan los olores para decirse cosas. Para encontrar alimento, siguen los olores dejados por otras hormigas.

hive/colmena

Bees also use smells to tell each other things. Honeybees give off different scents. They use the scents to know what jobs they should do in the hive.

- - - - - - - -

Las abejas también usan los olores para decirse cosas. Las abejas de la miel desprenden distintos olores. Usan los olores para saber qué trabajo deben hacer en la colmena.

An eel must use its sense of smell when it hunts. Eels cannot see very well.

▬ ▬ ▬ ▬ ▬ ▬ ▬ ▬

La anguila tiene que usar su sentido del olfato cuando caza. Las anguilas no pueden ver muy bien.

Moles cannot see well, either. Like an eel, a mole uses its sense of smell to find food.

— — — — — — — —

Los topos tampoco ven bien. Como la anguila, el topo usa su sentido del olfato para encontrar comida.

Many animals have strong scents. They sniff each other to find out if they are from the same family.

- - - - - - - -

Muchos animales despiden olores fuertes. Se olisquean unos a otros para saber si son de la misma familia.

Many animals use their sense of smell when they hunt for food. Smells also warn animals of danger and help them stay alive in the wild.

— — — — — — — —

Muchos animales salvajes usan su sentido del olfato cuando buscan comida. Los olores los advierten del peligro y los ayudan a sobrevivir.

Glossary

hive — a home for honeybees

nostrils — the outer openings of the nose

prey — animals that are hunted and killed by other animals for food

scents — certain smells or odors

Glosario

colmena — casa de las abejas

fosas nasales — aberturas externas de la nariz

presa — animal que otros animales cazan para alimentarse

For More Information/Más información

Books

Animal Noses. Look Once, Look Again (series).
David M. Schwartz (Gareth Stevens)

Smelling in Living Things. Karen Hartley, Chris Macro,
and Philip Taylor (Heinemann Library)

Libros

Elephants/Los elefantes. Animals I See at the Zoo/
Animales que veo en el zoológico (series).
JoAnn Early Macken (Weekly Reader Early Learning Library)

Los perros/Dogs.
Jennifer Blizin Gillis (Heinemann)

Index

Índice

About the Author

Kirsten Hall is an author and editor. While she was still in high school, she published her first book for children, *Bunny, Bunny*. Since then she has written and published more than eighty titles. A former teacher, Kirsten currently spends her days writing and editing and her evenings tutoring. She lives in New York City with her husband.

Información sobre la autora

Kirsten Hall es escritora y editora. Publicó su primer libro para niños, *Bunny, Bunny,* cuando aún asistía a la escuela secundaria. Desde entonces, ha escrito y publicado más de ochenta títulos. Kirsten, que anteriormente fue maestra, pasa el día escribiendo y editando, y por la noche da clases. Kirsten vive en la ciudad de Nueva York con su esposo.